God's Miracle-
a Seed

Rebecca Newswanger

Christian Light Publications, Inc.
Harrisonburg, Virginia 22802

GOD'S MIRACLE—A SEED

Christian Light Publications, Inc., Harrisonburg, Virginia 22802
©2004 by Christian Light Publications, Inc.
Printed in the United States of America

3rd Printing, 2011

Artist: Harold Weaver

ISBN 978-0-87813-620-9

God's Miracle-
a Seed

Look! here's a tiny grain of corn;
  Inside is God's surprise;
For no one else could make a seed
  But our great God so wise!

The farmer plows the deep, dark earth,
    Before the winter storm.
The soil awaits beneath the snow
    Till springtime makes it warm.

And when God's sun with gentle rays
Has dried the waiting ground,
The farmer gets his tractor out.
Oh, what a roaring sound!

He pulls his disk and harrow 'round
  To make the dark soil fine,
So he can plant the grains of corn
  In straight and length'ning line.

And now we'll watch one little seed
    To see our big surprise.
For God will work a miracle
    Of growth before our eyes.

The blue, blue sky is spread above
  The rich, brown earth below.
And snug within its moist, warm bed,
  The kernel starts to grow.

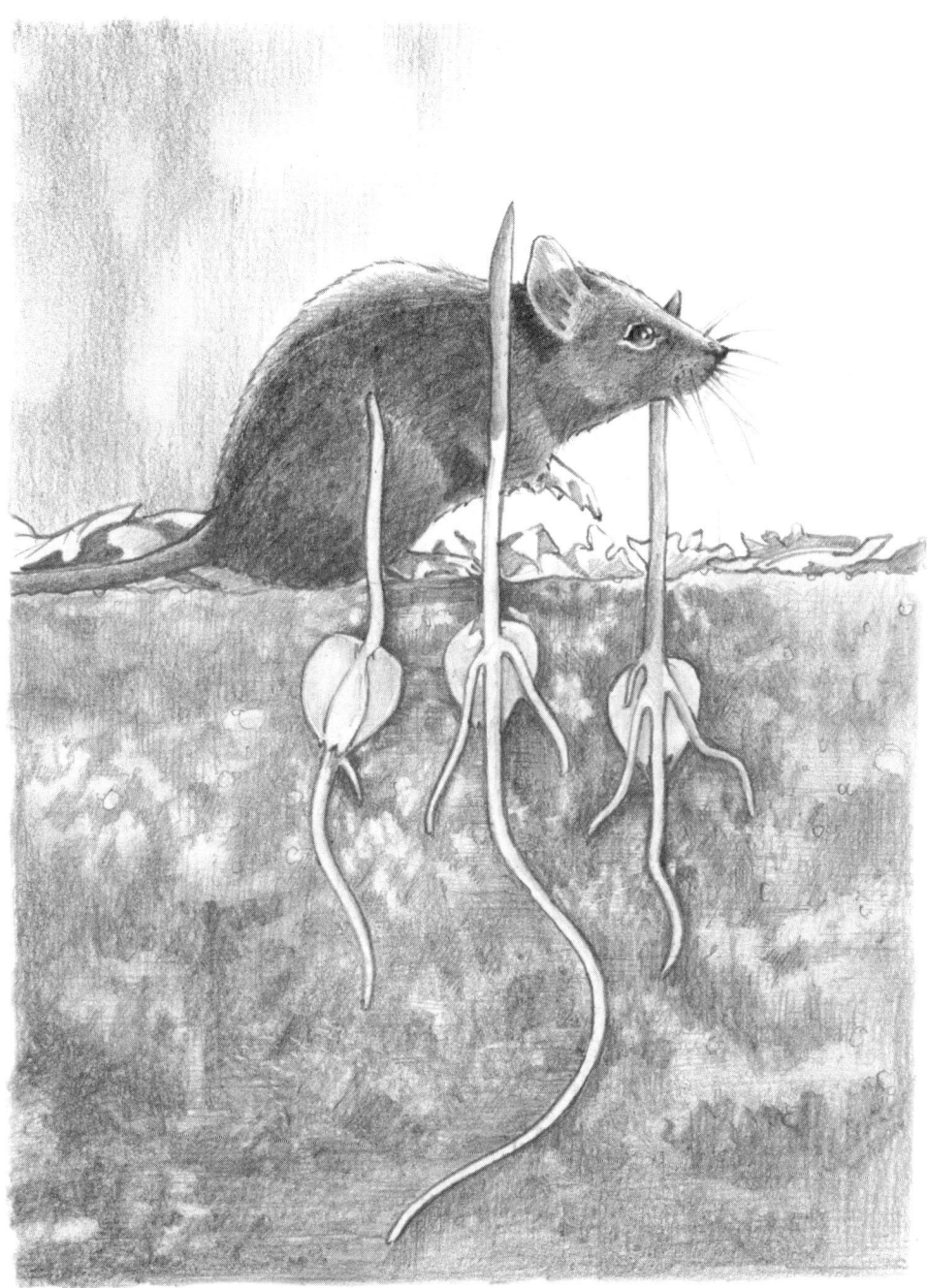

The tiny seed swells big and fat;
    A plump root pushes down.
Up, up—a little spear of green
    Bursts forth above the ground.

Splish! Splash! God's rain falls to the
earth
    And dampens all the soil.
The farmer must destroy the weeds
    With hard and steady toil.

Two little leaves will soon unfold
From out the tiny spear.
And as the summer days pass on,
More leaves, and more, appear.

Out pops a tassel on the top;
   Our stalk is tall and strong.
And all around us through the leaves,
   We hear the wind's soft song.

Look! Every stalk of corn around
    Hugs tight a growing ear.
Soft silk a-flutters from the top;
    Soon grains will grow in here.

We watch the summer flowers fade,
    As children go to school.
Our stalk has changed from green to
brown,
    While nights are turning cool.

The tiny ear grew big and brown.
   Now through the drying husk,
Straight rows of golden grains shine
bright
   In ev'ning's gath'ring dusk.

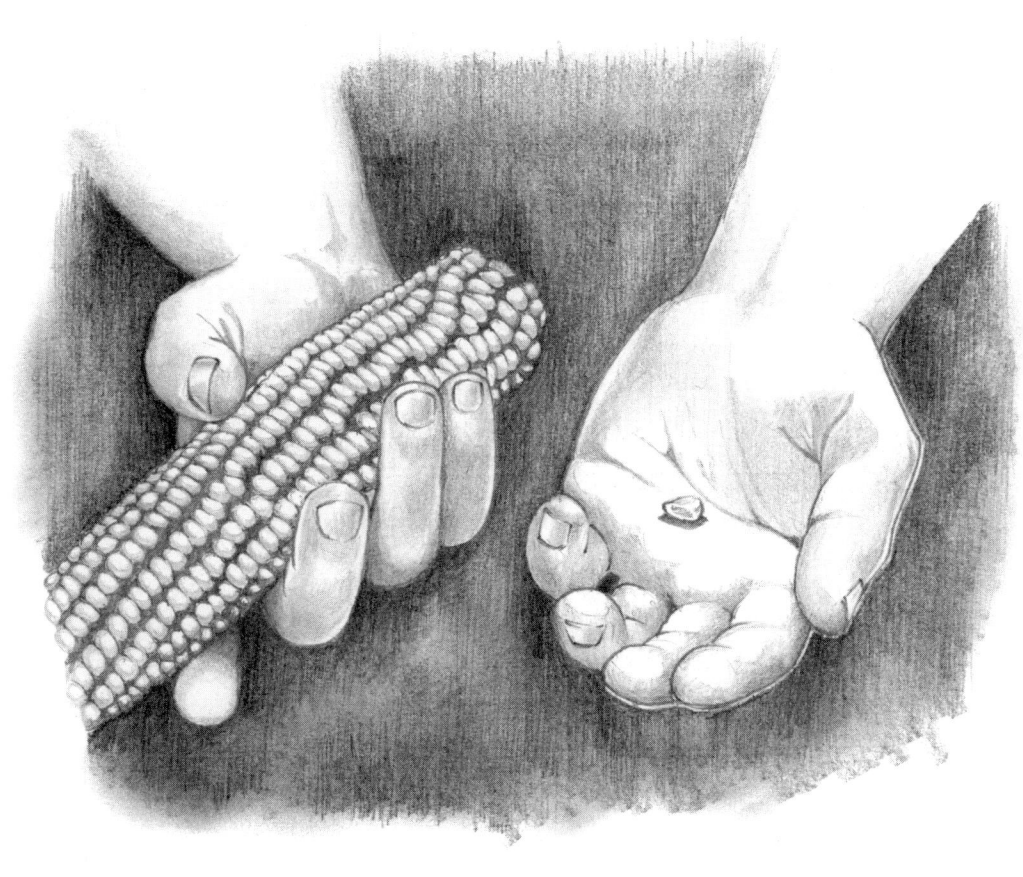

Just think of how that mighty stalk
   Grew out of one small seed.
And it produced these lovely grains—
   A miracle indeed.

The farmer brings his combine now,
 To shell the golden corn.
A yellow stream fills waiting bins;
 The field looks clipped and shorn.

This winter, cows will eat the corn
    The farmer grinds—and then
We'll wait until next spring to watch
    God's miracle again.

Christian Light Publications, Inc., is a nonprofit, conservative Mennonite publishing company providing Christ-centered, Biblical literature including books, Gospel tracts, Sunday school materials, summer Bible school materials, and a full curriculum for Christian day schools and homeschools. Though primarily produced in English, some books, tracts, and school materials are also available in Spanish.

For more information about the ministry of CLP or its publications, or for spiritual help, please contact us at:

Christian Light Publications, Inc.
P. O. Box 1212
Harrisonburg, VA 22803-1212

Telephone—540-434-0768
Fax—540-433-8896
E-mail—info@clp.org
www.clp.org